Breadfruit

Breadfruit

Janet London Stewart

XULON PRESS

Xulon Press
2301 Lucien Way #415
Maitland, FL 32751
407.339.4217
www.xulonpress.com

© 2018 by Janet London Stewart

All rights reserved solely by the author. The author guarantees all contents are original and do not infringe upon the legal rights of any other person or work. No part of this book may be reproduced in any form without the permission of the author. The views expressed in this book are not necessarily those of the publisher.

Scripture quotations taken from the New King James Version (NKJV). Copyright © 1982 by Thomas Nelson, Inc. Used by permission. All rights reserved.

Printed in the United States of America.

ISBN-13: 9781545624081

Table of Contents

Sion Hill/St Vincent 1
Uncle Ed 3
A Summer's Day in- Bequia 4
Spiritual Food 6
Paradise-Island. 7
Hurricane-Janet. 8
 Macaroni and Cheese 9
Daydream 10
Aunt -Millie 12
Mom a – Reviere. 13
Quietude. 14
Inspiration 15
Ode to Sajel 16
The Wind 17
God 18
Stone Mountain 19
Wind Song 20
M-a- n-d-e-l-a 21
Winter Tree 22
St Vincent Paradise -Island 23
The Company of Crickets. 24
Me- My Book -My Coffee 25
Mrs. Rain 26
Aunt Mable 27

Janet London Stewart

Aunt Millie...................................29
Ambien......................................30
The World Needs a Hug........................32
PLG-Prospect Lefferts Garden 33
Spotty Dog...................................34
Blue Depression Cloud........................36
Daydream.....................................37

Sion Hill/St Vincent

I left my childhood behind to find the streets paved with gold
Sion Hill was everything to me
My life my hope my everything
Have you ever been to Sion Hill?
Back to the place I left behind?
If not-Please do! Please do!
Visit!
You must! You must!
You can see, where the blue green of the ocean meet
the horizon
The sight, sound and smell of the ocean air will
relax and comfort you
Listening to the waves lapping against the sea shore will mesmerize you with the rhythmic sounds of Beans and Antipop
See the birds high in the air, flying towards far-off islands
Watch imposing, breathtaking, mountains views and goats
grazing on grassy hills
Coconut trees with their spreading fronds will supply cool
shade while you fill your tummy with the coconut jelly, drink
delicious, and nutritious coconut water
Through the window you will be engulfed by the scent
of ripe mangoes, papaya, bananas, sugar-apples, damsels,
and red plums
You will join with the natives in the making of
guava cheese and guava jelly
The marketplace will intoxicate you, with all the
tropical fruits and provisions
The old men will tell you folktales and Nancy stories.

continued

Janet London Stewart

Be warned!!
After you hear, the Calypso music played by the
Mighty Sparrow, Kitchener and Lord Melody
You can dance and wine your bodyline in the streets
of Kingstown
Is it possible to reach those days again?

Uncle Ed

E- for short
I left you on the Antilles, all alone
Down on the island where it always shine
Time flew while I was gone
As a child
You treated me like your kin
You picked up the pieces
My father left behind
He walked away and never turned back
He never turned back
He never turned back
You filled the black hole
He fed my dry blistered soul
With kindness, and compassion like Jesus did for Bartimaeus
You wiped my tears when I felt sad and lonely
You gave me medicinal herbs for my queasy tummy
Castrol oil and ginger tea was the cure
You dried my tears and turned them into smiles
At times when I thought I heard my papa's voice
I looked up, saw your reassuring smile-it gave me
courage to move on
The expression I saw in your cinnamon nutmeg eyes
You kind words and infectious smile
Said to me: That's my girl
You reproached me when I disobeyed the rules my mama set
I hung my head in shame, for I wanted you to be proud of me
I am so sorry I didn't have the chance to see you again
To tell you how much I loved you so, and still do
Many, many things left unsaid, so many,
many unanswered questions
I will see you again dear Uncle Eddie.

A Summer's Day in- Bequia

Their journey began when they boarded the ship Madadina
He walked over to her with a twinkle in his eyes
He stretched out his hand, took hers kissing it gently, and softly
He looked at her lovingly, bowed his head and offered her a
bunch of ripe sea grapes, Picked from
Megan's bay that morning
The succulent taste of the grapes awakened her palate
She tiptoed closer to him
They held each other in a warm embrace,
enjoying the reflective rays of the tropical sun
They drank, cold Mauby and Gingerbeer
She looked at him, beamed from ear to ear
Like a giddy sixteen year old school girl
As the sun went down, and the evening chill came
The moon floated across the powdered blue sky
They remained lost in the fantasy of the day
Until
Startled by the Conch whistle of the fishermen three
They dived into the blue tortoise waters of the Caribbean Sea
And disappeared.

Mommy/Gone too soon

A Nubian Queen she was
A sophisticated brown –skinned lady was a beauty to behold
When she walked up the street
Men gazed, gawked and blushed
Women shook their heads and wanted to imitate her
Children moved up close, and wanted to hold her hand
Why? Her dark brown eyes invited them to
the doorway of her heart
Gone too soon- Gone too soon
All your children, and grandchildren each of them
have something of you
Your eyes, your smile, your strength, your ambition, your
tenacity and your spirit
So mom you are still with us?
Gone too soon!
Gone too soon!!

Spiritual Food

Suffering from despair, frustration, distress, and spiritual hunger
I Know
It's like pieces of rocks being pushed deeper and
deeper into your wounded flesh
Do you know?
Mankind cannot survive without spiritual food

Why?
It gives hope to the broken-hearted, the mentally ailing,
and the desperate
How does spiritual food taste

Want to know?
Buttery, fruit, yummy, chocolatey, savory, decadent
and full of gustatory sensations

It will whet your appetite sharpen your senses and
stimulate your desire for more

It awakens a craving in your soul while satisfying and
strengthening your soul
You will know about this spiritual food

Only by reading the Bible
Following and practicing Bible principles

You can satisfy your hunger for spiritual food

Paradise-Island

Enjoying the beautiful and serene June morning
With a twinkle in their eyes and
He kissed her hands softly and gently
You could hear her heart beat thump! thump!
She was at peace no more darkness no more pain
They lazed on the glorious Argyle bay, surrounded by
the volcano and glittering black sand
In the distance tourist ship sailed from island
Calypso and Ragee music filled the air with the tropical
sounds of the Mighty Sparrow, Lord Kitchener, and Melody
Through the waves were high their souls rocked
backward and forward
Nesting their toes into the sand and the sea spraying their bodies
The sea spraying their legs and the san
The enjoyment of the blue-green water added bliss to
the tranquility of the day
The lost their bodies to the healing of the sea
They threw their bodies to the healing of the sea.

Hurricane-Janet

Hurricane Janet in 55 rushed to the shores of St. Vincent Island
Oh mercy! Oh mercy!
Granny gritted her teeth in fear
Before she can blink an eye
Her world, her island was turned upside down
Palm trees shuddered
Fear tore at every branch and root
Granny barred the windows
Nailed the doors shut with 10inch nails
Run to the cellar, children
Guided by the old kerosene lamp they descended the stairs
Down, they scampered with granny on their heels
They huddled like hibernating bears
Consoling the ones who needed to
Shivers, and moans, you can hear them groan
Granny hugged her grandchildren together,
and lovingly protected them from the howling hurricane
The blue skies lay buried under the dark black clouds
Coconuts fell in unison, each one hugging the other for survival
Hurricane Janet. Oh! Mercy on us
More branches, and trees fell, and smashed into pieces
The roosters, hens, and chickens flew their coops and landed
in the pig's pen, only to be greeted by Oink! Oink! Oink!
The rain tapered into a drizzle
The trees stretched, and smiled
Granny's praise to the Lord broke the stillness of the morning
Finally peace at last.

Macaroni and Cheese

Water- water
Serve serve- serve
Malcolm: Hot, hot, hot
Uncle Bert blow, blow, blow
Daddy; be patient be patient
Malcolm: Cool, cool, cool. He blows eyes
wide open with excitement
Malcolm: Taste taste tantalize
Malcolm: Yummy, yummy
Yielding to his senses
The hot- cooling macaroni and cheese
He finally succumbed to their encouraging words.

Daydream

Lying in bed, my cheeks huddled gently against
LBT comfortable pillow
I stared at the annoying clock with purple digital numbers
At the damage mismatched orange and blue ceiling design
Longing to sleep, but my eyes are at open and tingling
I could smell and taste the stillness of the room
I inhaled the bitter sweet pungent odor of mauby
It wafted through my room overpowering me
with every breath I took
It affected my ear drums, and I thought it
would burst into fragments
I could hear the rush of my breath, my heart beating fast
My perception is now out of focus
My head becomes a late night bizarre TV station
Listening to little snips of songs, and pep talk from Letterman
A pit of swirling darkness surrounds me
Panicking
I took the last two pills that would take me into an Ambien haze
I wrapped my body into a turtle-like shell
Readying for the journey
It is moments like these, that the grey universe
claims my body and my soul
The phenomenon happens: I fall asleep
This night for reasons unknown the A hits harder than usual
I wander aimlessly through the clouds
In my mental confusion and zombie-like state
In my mystic radiance
I stretched out my hands, and fingers
Dreaming. I floated inside the cocoon of warmth and safety
Far away from the paradoxical effects of Ambien

Breadfruit

Mom appeared
Her loving eyes flashed to mine, she nodded
I saw the tears shimmering in her ebony eyes
She waved goodbye

Aunt -Millie

Through the years I have thought about you
The love we shared the memories too
I had to leave with no good bye
Always feeling a sense of loss for my dearest aunt Millie
How can I possibly thank you?
Everywhere you went you trailed a cloud of youthfulness and strength
You were exuberant with the enthusiasm of a teenager
The one who gave me toys ginger sticks sugar cake, and my very first baby doll house with all the trimmings
Please forgive my self-centeredness
For as I approach my golden years
I realize I should have kept in touch with you
My dearest, dearest aunt Millie
The best friend of my mother dear and me
Again, please forgive my selfishness
To me you were a second mom
The person I drew wisdom from
Regrets are daggers in my soul
I am tormented and wounded like a knife that have been plunged into my heart
Where the bleeding never stops
Sadness and frustration, just a step away
To cope to muddle through life
I still like to play make believe
Especially when she baked rum cake and bread pudding - soaked in coconut milk and served with a guava rum sauce.
After Sunday school magical
See you again, Aunt Millie.

Mom a – Reviere

Surrounded by white satin sheets as she did every night for the past five years. Marie was struck by the sheer beauty and luxury that surrounded her in her bedroom.

She lay on a Duxiana bed between the pales of lavender sateen sheets under a light pink quilt that had been handmade by her granny. She slept with the window open, the scent of oranges from the trees outside wafted through the air.

It was serene. So serene. It struck her a new every morning when she woke up. This was where she lived now fifteen minutes from her old house. She closed her eyes, body stiffened and fell asleep.

In her rem cycle she saw Jehovah with his hands stretched out surrounded by angels and the brightest light she had ever seen. They reflected glittering shades of blue, red and gold they consumed her.

A warm glow permeated her body and soul. She lay transfixed until she felt her body move to a place of wonder. I reached out to touch his hand. He quietly and purposely moved away. In an instant she woke with tears in her eyes and a heavy heart.

She felt calm, peaceful and tranquil as if she was in the sound of her spirit.

Quietude

Surrounded by green satin sheets
Staring at the exotic painting of Madonna
The house was absolutely silent you could hear a pin drop
Light oozing from the room came from the brightly lit candles
The flames flickered back and forth, back and forth casting
shadows on the pink walls and bedpost
Confused, helpless
She opened the window
The wind blew in the cold
Hearing the songs of angels chanting
Only in her head
Body stiffened, she fell asleep
In her rem cycle she saw Jehovah
His hands stretched out
He was encircled by the brightest lights she had ever seen
They reflected, glittering shades of blue, sapphire, purple,
yellow, gold and green
A warm glow penetrated her soul
Transfixed until she felt her body move to a place of wonder
He smiled and cautiously and purposely moved away
In an instant she awoke with tears of joy in her heart.
She felt strangely calm as she woke up with a surge of elation
She had her mind back.

Inspiration

Praying for an answer. A few moments later this is what came to be... Sometimes when we cannot see our own uniqueness and purpose there is always something right around the corner to remind us that we all have a purpose in this life... We just have to sometimes sit still and listen to the small faint whisper within...

Ode to Sajel

The thuds, clunks, crashes coupled with the echo of her voice
Soothes you into a carefully crafted spell
She is like a Caribbean flying-fish making, self-propelled leaps
Out of water into air
She perches head in hand like a humming bird, along the
rickety, wrought-iron bedrail of her grandma's bed
She gazes into grandma's dark brown ebony eyes
While she read her bible -a new scriptural verse every night
There on her face are tears as she read
Not tears of sorrow, but tears of joy
The sight of her grandma's kind face
Softened with age and wrinkles, always made her feel better
She snuck into her Grandma's bed curled up
near the edge of the bed
And gazed into the deep clear watery walls of grandma's heart
Oh Grandma!! Oh Grandma!! She whispered
Sleeping with you makes me feel comfortable and safe
You smell like ginger curry, maze, and lavender too
Closing her eyes wide shut while she savoring the
pungent smells coming from her flannel nightie
Draping herself around the sheets
She floats away losing herself in the rhythm of the clouds
Sleep my lovely until the sun is gone
Until the sun is gone.

The Wind

She is sensitive and caring
Like the hands of Malcolm, Langston and Baby Dean
She gallops like Sanura, and Rie
Into the tropical rain forest
She dances with the flow of the waves
Holding them ripple by ripple prancing around like a mermaid
Whistling to the musical lyrics of the Caribbean
Like Sajel.

God

You have designed us for good works- Ephesians 2:10
Our purpose is to love you, glorify you
Be obedient to you
And love thy neighbor as thyself
You look down from Heaven
Shake your head when we do silly things
Have a twinkle in your eyes
When we say the model prayer
You smile with us, when we imitate you
You are happy when we gather with spirit-minded humans
And we know "for sure" it makes you happy and happy
When we love and forgive one another
Because we are preparing ourselves for Paradise on earth
Oh Jehovah help your imperfect children- Till as a river flows our peace
Your word certainly will build up those who study and employ it in their lives!

Stone Mountain

Lent to us by God Almighty
A massive height in Georgia State
This monument of stone have seen countless days
She stands awe inspiring and majestic
Built by our ancestors sweating, slogging and toiling
She walks alone. Against the bluest of skies and starry stars
Greeting them with a royal bow
She looks below at the mere mortals
Who have climbed her through the years,
fascinated by her presenced
To Me
The beguiling presence of this mountain
filtered through my bones
All 200 of them
Making them quiver filling every bone, and cell with solace
As I reached the top
In a light stroking gesture
She caressed my bones expressing affection
She ignited energy through the fleshy part of my face
Nature's peace flowed into me like sunshine flows into trees
Wrapping myself into the moment
I close my eyes formed a mental image
And pay homage to my ancestors
This coarse grain crystalline textured light red granite
Hard igneous rock
Provoked me with wonder, and inspired my inquisitive longing
Should I have made the mountain my home**?**

Wind Song

The wind blew cold through the opened window

Shivered at the cool breeze she forced herself to descend
She mumbled as she glanced down at the
immensity of the big oak
Briefly scrutinizing its gnarled and leafless branches
Hoping the tree's bulk will lessen the ferocity of any further wind
Suddenly she heard the songs of angels chanting
But they were only in her head
She closed my eyes, her body stiffened, then she fell asleep
In her rem cycle she saw Jehovah
His hands stretched out
He was encircled by the brightest lights she had ever seen
They reflected, glittering shades of blue, sapphire, purple,
yellow, gold and green
A warm glow penetrated her soul
Transfixed until she felt her body move to a place of wonder
He smiled and cautiously and purposely moved away
In an instant she awoke with tears of joy in her heart.
She felt strangely calm as she woke up with a surge of elation
She had her mind back.

M-a- n-d-e-l-a

Troubled souls, he led
Brighten our universe and teach us a thing or two or three, he did
He understood our shortcomings
He changed the course of history
We miss you, we miss you
Your spirit is here forever in our hearts
And we are here to honor you
M-a-n-d-e-l-a, M-a-n-d-e-la
You were friend and ancestral father,
Man of peace, courage, good judgment and honesty
They caged you like a cornered animal
They couldn't hold you down
Man of faith man of hope
Those bars were made of hate not love
But through your suffering pain and humiliation
You conquered and came out stronger than before
You became Lord of the manor
Through your graciousness and forgiving spirit
You loved your tormentors and gave them a space in your heart
Only Mandela! Only Mandela

Winter Tree

Winter tree winter tree
The Great Creator takes care of you
Your trunk clothed with shades of white and grey
You rise high above the hills, winding rivers and streams
He makes the winter sky clear and bright for you
With the music of the wind and the silence of the stars
He gives you a reassuring smile
Your leaves have turned brown
Your branches have withered down
Your twigs have weakened facedown
And thus they fall to the ground
He allows you the grace and freedom of the forest
So you can reflect on your memories of yesteryear
You are awake while creation is asleep
You see and hear every sound
You enjoy your nightly solitude
Until the rising of the sun
So winter tree winter tree
The Almighty will never let you down.

St Vincent Paradise -Island

The glorious Argyle bay lay calm, and beautiful in the
October sunshine

They lazed on the black volcanic glittering sand where the dense
smoke completely shrouded the summit of the mountain

In the vastness vessels came and went like chasing dreams

Some slowly disappearing like clouds that change
from gold to gray

Some sped more quickly like birds that seek their mother's nest
They listened to the musical orchestra of the world above
The sea spraying their legs and the sand tingling their feet

They felt a passion running through their veins

Like the power of the sea

Sending a salty taste to their tongues.

The Company of Crickets

Company of Crickets
The sweet sounds slips through my open window
Listening to the orchestral sounds of crickets through the trees

The crickets kept a tune that blanketed the air
Like the sounds of Beans and Antipop

The velvety night breeze took me on a spiritual quest
The crickets serenaded/crooned and entertain me

With an enchanting love song
The morning birds flying from tree to tree
branch to branch, leaf to leaf
Showing off their skills

A new day was dawning
The sky portrayed three shades of blue and two shades of gray
The Crickets danced, danced celebrating the new day

The flowers, plants, foliage all coming together
The taught me to appreciate the wonderful universe
We human inhabit.

Me- My Book -My Coffee

Me
Who am I?
Here in -44
Painfully shy as a child
Easy to get along with
Incredibly warm
Here in -2017

My Book
Spend every day
Writing & Editing
It gives me joy
It gives me peace
Keeps me away from the outside world
The lines reflect my life, they are all true

My Coffee
Mouth felt and tasteful
Stirs my brain
Stimulate my taste buds
The first sip hit my lips, and come alive
Like the first taste of a kiss

Mrs. Rain

Oh dear Oh dear
Never-ending drizzle
Birds shrieking, screaming sounding like
blood curdling screams of a helpless child
Trees humbly bowing their heads respectfully mumbling
Oh! Oh!. We need you Mrs. Rain
The homeless waif
Raises both hands in prayer connecting with her creator
Closing her eyes, she inhale exhale
Feeling the sparkling, crisp drop of pearls
Caressing, and bathing her ebony skin
It was as if every cell in her tired body had come alive
In the excitement
She began dancing and prancing to the
lyrical sounds of Vernon Reid
As he skillfully played his guitar
Her troubles are washed away
They meandered like a river into the depths of her soul
She feels complete and free like the Robin flying overhead
Enjoying the peaceful tranquility and nourishment from above
The richness, and love Mrs. Rain's showered on her,
made her feel safe.

Aunt Mable

I visited my Aunt Mable at the age of 9-1955 was the year
She lived above the coastline on the tropical island of St. Vincent
A dedicated matron and nurse was she
A friend of the lepers she always was
She nursed them as if they were her own
Faith, compassion humility and love guided her
One day she took me to visit them
Hoping I would follow in her footsteps
With dread and nervousness I went
Outside their cells, the walls were painted lily white
Inside the walls were dark and gray
Locked in their cells their arms out-stretched
Waiting to touch the skin of a humankind
Skin hunger they craved like you and me
Trapped in their scourged bodies
Fighting to get out, screaming for mercy and compassionate
You can hear souls crying, groaning wailing like animals in a cage
Challenged by the terror of their appearance
The stench of feces and foul urine tainted the air
Feces covered the side of the walls
The disease eating away at their extremities one by one
I saw their boil ridden bodies
Their fingers and toes can feel no pain
Some already have disappeared
My emotions stirred I was moved to sadness and tears
She picked them up and showed them care
Even sharing in their sorrows
Without the love she had for them, God only knows
where they would be

continued

Janet London Stewart

    She kindly asked her children say hello to my niece
        They looked at me smiled and nodded,
    I could see the twinkle in their half-closed eyes
Hearing the helpful and familiar voice of Aunt Mable
        brought them to their feet
    That day changed my life, and shaped my soul
It was Jehovah's wisdom revealed so brilliantly in Aunt Mable
      That changed my life forever.

Aunt Millie

In my youth you loved me so
1944 to 1965 you comforted me
I left you behind, I never looked back
1965 I migrated to the land of opportunity
And the home of the brave
My regret, and bitterness have left a distressing feeling in my heart
I adopted another culture and left my own
Before my passport to heaven runs out
My heart needed to say
You were the one
Who gave me toys, ginger sticks, sugar cakes,
my first doll house to?
Cooking Caribbean cuisine at the age of eight
Watching Carnival festivities from your window
Experiencing the raucous dance, pounding music and flamboyant costumes that makes up the celebration
Understanding African mysticism
Prepare and bake rum cake and bread pudding
soaked in coconut milk
You taught me well
For as I approach my golden years
I realize I should have kept in touch with
My dearest, most beloved aunt Millie
The best friend of my dear mother and me
Again, please forgive my selfishness
For my soul is tortured my flesh is weak
See you again Aunt Millie
Images of you will live in my heart forever.

Ambien

Cheeks nestled against the DIY pillow
Staring at the irritating clock loaded with red
digital crooked numbers
The damage mix matched numbers
orange and blue ceiling wallpaper
Longing to sleep, but my eyes are open and burning
A pungent smell filled my nostrils, and interrupted my thoughts
I inhaled, the bitter sweet pungent odor
It overpowered every breath I took
It augmented my ear drums, and I thought
they would burst into fragments
I could hear the rush of my breath, my heart beating fast
Temporary state of consciousness reared its ugly head
My head becomes a late night bizarre TV station
Listening to snippets of songs, and pep talk from Letterman
Oh! Oh! A pit of swirling darkness surrounded me
The hollowness I feel is unimaginable
Panicking
I took the last two pills that would get me into an Ambien haze
I wrapped my body in a turtle-like shell
Readying for the journey
It is moments like these that the gray universe claims
my body and soul
The phenomenon happens: I fall asleep
This night for reasons unknown A hits harder than usual
I wandered aimless aimlessly through the cloud
In my mental confusion and Zombie like state
In my mystic radiance, I stretched out my hand and fingers
Dreaming. I floated inside a cocoon of warmth and safety
Far away from the paradoxical effects of Ambien

Breadfruit

Mom! Mom! I cried out. She appeared in a white gown
She leaned her head back and looked at me
I felt the warm tears as they landed on my hand
Her dark brown eyes turned at me with surprise and concern
She walked away knowing I would be all right.

The World Needs a Hug

Thou messenger of love
Strong, majestic, regal, noble, and passionate
You stood
Nestled among the palm, coconut, mango, breadfruit,
sapodilla and oak trees
You were there
Fern, shrubs, and flowers
Embraced you
Animals of all species
Appreciated you
People of all shapes, sizes, and color
Respected you
Your calm loving and peaceful soul
Never failed
You embraced it all
Sins of omission thoughts, words, and deeds have taken over
You kept turning the pages of life, hoping you can
make a difference that would bind us once more
Hear my plea!
Aching, scratching my bald head till it bleeds
Due to a lack of a hug from you
My eyes are teary, my heart is despondent
All you ever needed was a hug
So hug the world, hug, hug, hug
Be confident
Don't be disappointed
Humankind will come around.

PLG-Prospect Lefferts Garden

Customers walk, run, skip, bike, baby stroller to PLG
Through the fury of the wind, and sleet
Like subway traffic in New York Penn station
They stumble out of their homes, apartments and hotels
Forming a line similar to subway traffic in Grand Central
To enjoy moments of culinary bliss
A divine atmosphere welcomes you, and you become friends
with two or three or four strangers
Eclectic paintings submitted by patrons adorn the walls
Wow!
Dining and eating your belly full is not an understatement
Playing burst of songs and rap lyrics by Beans add
to the feel good aura
So close your eyes inhale exhale, breathe that cuisine
into your central channel and allow it to permeate
Pastries from Colson you can't just eat one
Hudson Valley Bread Alone need no butter, maybe jelly
So Drink up! Eat up!
Pay no attention to the world swirling around you
The secret lies in peace, harmony, atmosphere, and good eats
Move over Alton Brown
All the comforting smells and scents will follow you home.

Spotty Dog

Customers, visitors
From somewhere and everywhere
Scurry like ants
Scamper like new-born puppies
To visit Spotty Dog a book and ale cafe
A looking for a reason to make them feel all right
Stumbling upon this café entrenched in Hudson valley history
Oh la la!
I took a seat
Smelled eats
My nostrils picked up the scent of ale and new books
Scents mixed with laughter, music, and food wafted from the café into the street
Caught up in the excitement and the moment
Your trouble will take a back seat
Drawn by the vanilla smell coming from the other side of the café
Aww! Books
Thumbing through the pages
And
Reading the new found books I wanted to crawl into a corner of a book and live there
They had become a part of me
The fifties, sixties and seventies magical poetic penned verses
Consuming the assortment of American ales with their tantalizing flavors gave me a buzz of a lifetime
Munching substantial plates of diced cheeses, Goat, American, Yellow Cheddar, and Brie surrounded by water, and whole wheat crackers
Was a wondrous journey for my taste buds

Breadfruit

Feeling out of myself and powerful
I left my spirits sky high
Until next time, until next time
Spotty Dog.

Blue Depression Cloud

Maneuvering and zigzagging my way across the
picturesque scenic and rural American countryside
I sense something was amiss
Lo and behold
Something specular came floating into my life
I looked up and saw the most beautiful powdered
depression blue cloud
Staring down at me
I asked" What's the matter cloud?
"You have a sad expression"
He said "I feel lonely there are no powdered blue depression
cloud to keep me company, and play hide and go seek
I said "Don't worry I am here beside you"
I exclaimed, "You are the most beautiful and rare
powdered blue depression cloud in the sky"
He smile shyly but his eyes shone
I said
"You look like a big ball of cotton"
"I could see you with my eyes wide shut
You are resilience, warm, kind and loving
You adapt to the shape of a Caribbean island
The face of Lena Horne and Patti Labelle

Daydream

Lying in bed, my cheeks huddled gently against LBT comfort-
able pillow
I stared at the annoying clock with purple digital numbers
At the damage mismatched orange and blue ceiling design
Longing to sleep, but my eyes are at open and tingling
I could smell and taste the stillness of the room
I inhaled the bitter sweet pungent odor of mauby
It wafted through my room overpowering me
with every breath I took
It affected my ear drums, and I thought it would
burst into fragments
I could hear the rush of my breath, my heart beating fast
My perception is now out of focus
My head becomes a late night bizarre TV station
Listening to little snips of songs, and pep talk from Letterman
A pit of swirling darkness surrounds me
Panicking
I took the last two pills that would take me into an Ambien haze
I wrapped my body into a turtle-like shell
Readying for the journey
It is moments like these, that the grey universe
claims my body and my soul
The phenomenon happens: I fall asleep
This night for reasons unknown the A hits harder than usual
I wander aimlessly through the clouds
In my mental confusion and zombie-like state
In my mystic radiance
I stretched out my hands, and fingers

continued

Janet London Stewart

Dreaming. I floated inside the cocoon of warmth and safety
Far away from the paradoxical effects of Ambien
Mom appeared
Her loving eyes flashed to mine, she nodded
I saw the tears shimmering in her ebony eyes
She waved goodbye

www.ingramcontent.com/pod-product-compliance
Ingram Content Group UK Ltd.
Pitfield, Milton Keynes, MK11 3LW, UK
UKHW041943230426
12048UKWH00008B/102